This book belongs to

. . . .

Reading with your child

Tips for sharing this book

Look at the front cover. What does your child think might happen in the story?

Talk about the back cover blurb. Why might the animals not all be able to get in the car together?

During reading

- Encourage your child to describe what is going on in the pictures.

- Ask them what is happening, and what they think might happen next.

- When you turn the page to see what actually happens, the outcome may or may not be what you expect! Talk about it.

- Give them lots of praise as you go along!

After reading

- Look at the back for some fun activities.

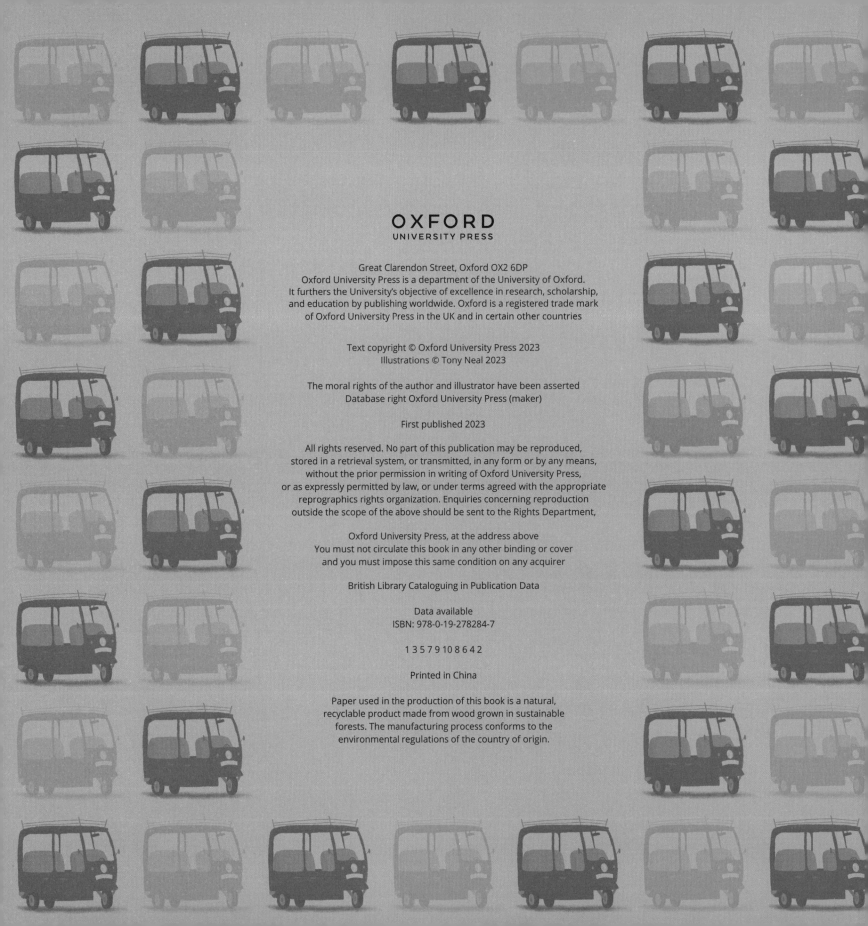

OXFORD
UNIVERSITY PRESS

Great Clarendon Street, Oxford OX2 6DP
Oxford University Press is a department of the University of Oxford.
It furthers the University's objective of excellence in research, scholarship,
and education by publishing worldwide. Oxford is a registered trade mark
of Oxford University Press in the UK and in certain other countries

British Library Cataloguing in Publication Data

Data available
ISBN: 978-0-19-278284-7

1 3 5 7 9 10 8 6 4 2

Printed in China

Paper used in the production of this book is a natural,
recyclable product made from wood grown in sustainable
forests. The manufacturing process conforms to the
environmental regulations of the country of origin.

TONY NEAL

SQUEEZE IN, SQUIRREL!

OXFORD
UNIVERSITY PRESS

Let's go!

Wait, my suitcase!

Is there room
for me?

Yes, it's empty.
Jump in, Mouse!

Here I come!

Is there room
for me?

Yes, jump in, Monkey!

Can I come too?

Yes, hop in, Frog!

No, there's lots of room!

It's fine.
Jump in,
Giraffe!

But what about me?!

I can help.
Jump in!

Ta da!

Activities

Capacity

These could be fun activities to do outside at a water table, or even in the bath!

Containers

Take a container, such as a cup or plastic bottle.

Challenge your child to make the container as **full** of water as they can, without spilling.

Can they make it **half full**? And **empty**?

How much does it hold?

Gather a selection of different-sized containers, such as a cup, a jug, and a bucket.

Ask your child which container holds the **most**, and which the **least**. Pour water between the containers to check.

As an extra challenge, find a **tall thin** container, and a **short wide** container. Which do they think will hold the **most** water? Are they surprised by the answer?